PRINTHOUSE BOOKS

PRESENTS

Inspirational Celebrity Short Stories

Inspirational

Angela Butler

VIP INK Publishing Group, Inc.

Atlanta, GA.

© 2015, by Angela Butler

PrintHouse Books

PrintHouseBooks.com

VIP INK Publishing Group, Incorporated

All rights reserved. No parts of this book may be reproduced in any way, shape or form or by any means without written permission from the publisher or the Author, except by a reviewer.

Printed in the USA

Cover art designed by Beyond Graphics.

Published: 3-1-2016

Isbn – 978-0-9970016-55

Editor: Shelby Oates

Library of Congress Cataloging-in-Publication Data

#2016930922

Angela Butler

1. Inspirational 2. Success

3. Celebrity   4. Angela Butler

Inspirational Celebrity Short Stories

Inspirational Celebrity Short Stories was taken from the hit radio show interview series "Show Talk with Angela Butler".

Angela Butler

This collection of short stories was written so that I could share the interviews from my hit radio show "Show Talk with Angela Butler" that are inspirational as well as enlightening. I hope all who read the selections are inspired and motivated. Each person included is unique regardless of status, but all are celebrities, some known within their cities and states and others known worldwide. They are all equally motivational who can inspire others with their life stories. I am glad and honored that these people graced my show and allowed me to interview them.

Inspirational Celebrity Short Stories

Table Contents

Chapter 1	Sarah Jakes	Page 10
Chapter 2	TNT Maddox	Page 12
Chapter 3	Yolanda Moore	Page 14
Chapter 4	Kevin W. Thornbourne	Page 15
Chapter 5	Shirley Murdock	Page 18
Chapter 6	Melba Moore	Page 19
Chapter 7	Lenny Williams	Page 20
Chapter 8	Johnathan Butler	Page 22
Chapter 9	The Force MD's	Page 24
Chapter 10	Rodney Perry	Page 26
Chapter 11	Damon Wayans, Jr.	Page 28
Chapter 12	Christine Houston	Page 30

Chapter 13	Paul Lamar Hunter	Page 33
Chapter 14	A. Morton/Miss Black America	Page 35
Chapter 15	Dr. Melanye Maclin	Page 37
Chapter 16	Kevin Bion Spencer	Page 39
Chapter 17	Vickie Winans	Page 41
Chapter 18	Harrison Page	Page 43
Chapter 19	Marc Gordon	Page 45
Chapter 20	Mayor J. Marks III	Page 47
Chapter 21	FL Senator Alfred Lawson, Jr.	Page 48
Chapter 22	Ted Lange	Page 50
Chapter 23	Andy Hilfiger	Page 52
Chapter 24	Dave Tolliver	Page 53
Chapter 25	Dr. Willie H. Bailey, Sr.	Page 56

Inspirational Celebrity Short Stories

Chapter 26	Dr. Walter Burns	Page 59
Chapter 27	Dr. Torri J. Evans-Barton	Page 61
Chapter 28	Att. Racquel Brown Gaston	Page 63
Chapter 29	Eddie Levert, Jr.	Page 65
Chapter 30	James H. Costen, Jr.	Page 67
Chapter 31	Quincy Bonds aka "Pookie"	Page 71
Chapter 32	GM Kraiguer Smith	Page 73
Chapter 33	Ready for the World	Page 75
Chapter 34	ANTWAN BANK$	Page 77
Chapter 35	Lennie Orwell	Page 79
Chapter 36	Carla Mills	Page 81
Chapter 37	Isabelle Doll-Ncogbo	Page 84
Chapter 38	Herman Dummon, Jr.	Page 86

Chapter 39	Willie T. Clay	Page 88
Chapter 40	Innocence Project	Page 90
Chapter 41	Maxwell Pickett	Page 92
Chapter 42	Bryan D. Barton	Page 95
Chapter 43	Jerrell Shearin	Page 99
Chapter 44	Andrea Hoosman	Page 101
Chapter 45	President D. Scott	Page 103
Chapter 46	Tamara Pray Frazier	Page 106
Chapter 47	Ricky Jason	Page 109
Chapter 48	Cordell Dean	Page 112

Chapter 1:

Sarah Jakes

Sarah Jakes is the daughter of Bishop TD Jakes; Sarah became a mother at a young age and she also married young. In spite of this, her famous father Bishop TD Jakes and his wife encouraged their daughter to succeed. They also stood by her and did not condemn her for the fact that she was so heavily committed at such an early stage in life.

Even though Sarah was a young mother who divorced quickly, she grew to become a woman of great character and strength. Sarah Jakes through her belief in God and her determination overcame her own personal trials and tribulations. This has only made her stronger and more dedicated to her children and also has made her a woman of great character.

Chapter 2:

TNT Maddox

TNT Maddox is the second female to play basketball for the Harlem Globe Trotters. She has opened the door for other females to join the team. TNT Maddox has accomplished much in her young life. She has toured the world with the famous Globe Trotters and has entertained many. She has also brought laughter and smiles too many lives because of the funny sayings and basketball antics the HGT perform on the basketball court for children and adults.

People of all ages enjoy watching them play and sometimes they even get to participate.

TNT Maddox inspires others by bringing joy and fun to many people.

Chapter 3:

Yolanda Moore

Yolanda Moore is one of the first females to play professional basketball in the Women's National Basketball Association (or the WNBA). Yolanda is the daughter of a single mother and didn't always have things easy in her life; she has had to fight for everything. But this has only made her stronger and more determined to achieve. Liking basketball changed her life and being tall most definitely helped because this sport is where she achieved and excelled the most. Yolanda dedicated so much of her energy and time to perfecting her game that she eventually earned a basketball scholarship for Ole Miss University.

While in college, Yolanda learned of the tryouts for the WNBA. At first, she was unfortunately discouraged from trying out by some of the people around her. But in spite of this she went to the tryouts anyway and was picked for the women's basketball draft. She is now the first African American coach of a Women's Class A basketball team in a private school in Mississippi. All of these slam dunks hurdling over adversity make Yolanda Moore a winner.

Chapter 4:

Kevin Wendell Thornbourne

Author Kevin Wendell Thornbourne is a gifted writer who vividly composes the civil rights movement within New York State. His book <u>The Life and Times of Kevin Wendell Thornbourne, Harlem Son</u>, is where he writes about the Black Power Movement of the 50's and 60's while also sharing knowledge about the World Trade Center bombings orchestrated by Bin Laden. Both experiences Kevin has lived through and, yes, survived.

Kevin has met Tipper Gore, the wife of Vice President Gore and Kevin's son and family were even invited to the White House for Sunday Dinner. His life has been spent mostly in Harlem, New York and he even has periods in his life here where he would see celebrities in their daily lives, people such as the Poet Langston Hughes who would speak at various schools in the area, Frankie Lymon and many more. Kevin Wendell Thornbourne is a living history book.

Chapter 5:

Shirley Murdock

Shirley Murdock is a soulful and talented singer who began singing when she was fifteen years old. She is known around the world for her songs: "As We Lay", "I Love Me Better Than That", and of course "The Lady, Her Lover, and Her Lord". These songs and many other songs have inspired millions of people. Shirley Murdock and her husband are now preachers who love to spread the word of God to millions. Shirley Murdock is an inspiration to many and at this point in her life she is saving souls for her Lord.

Chapter 6:

Melba Moore

Melba Moore is a singer and actress. She is well known for her soulful voice. She also won a 1970 Tony Award for best performance by a featured actress in a musical. She was nominated for a Grammy in 2014 and Moore has opened doors for many songstresses for whom she has paved the way. Despite her trials and tribulations she is a true survivor and is still going strong by helping and inspiring many.

Chapter 7:

Lenny Williams

Lenny Williams is a well renowned R&B singer, with hits like "'Cause I Love You". He also won a BMI Award with Kanye West for the song "Over Night Celebrity" in 2004 and 2005 which was recorded by rapper Twista. He is well known and famous for the song "Girl You Know".

Recently Lenny Williams has worked with Aretha Franklin, Alicia Keys, Anthony Hamilton, Bobby Womack and many others. His newer songs are" This is for the One That Got Away" and "Still". Lenny Williams has been wooing millions with his beautiful and unique voice for years. His songs have created romantic moments for so many. He is not just a legend, but has opened doors for hundreds, if not thousands and there is no sign of his trail blazing career coming to a halt any time soon.

Many have walked in his foot steps, but no one can walk in Lenny Williams' shoes as they are his and his alone.

Chapter 8:

Johnathan Butler

Johnathan Butler is a famous gospel singer who started singing in Athlone Cape Town, South Africa. Even though there was apartheid in Africa when he started out, he is one of the first artist's to have a crossover hit during this time. Thankfully he survived these dangerous years and he has recorded many songs about racial segregation to inform and heal. He also won the Sarie Award which is South Africa's equivalent to the Grammy.

Not only has he prevailed in spite of

racism he has also helped the people of Africa. The song that he is most famous for is "Falling in Love with Jesus". Not only can he sing, but he also writes, composes, and plays the acoustic guitar. Johnathan Butler has lived through apartheid and is still growing strong.

Chapter 9:

The Force MD's

The Force MD's are famous for the beautiful ballads: "Tender Love", "Love is a House", "Hear I Go Again" and of course "Tender Love". These ballads are timeless to many. On Show Talk with Angela Butler, The Force MD's even said, "President Obama listens to us on Air Force One on his iPod!"

The Force MD's are not just artists, but men who are role models for countless people. Their beautiful ballads are often sung at weddings. The Force MD's are known for contributions to the New Jack Swing Era and also to various urban categories with songs like "The Quiet Storm". The song "Tender Love" has been sampled by other a diversity of other artists which is a vast compliment for the group. Even though a few of the members are deceased, their beautiful voices and songs live on. The Force MD's songs actually are romance for diverse collectives of love birds.

Chapter 10:

Rodney Perry

Rodney Perry is a comedian and actor. His becoming a father while graduating from high school at the same time influenced him to go into the military. He spent eight years in the Navy. Even though he wanted to be a comedian, he knew he had to provide for his family. Acting and comedy were his passions though, so he decided not to enlist again once his first contract was completed.

As a standup comedian he experienced success and was living his dream. At one point he even met Oscar winner Monique which led him to be her co-host for her television show "The Monique Show". Millions of people knew him and his name.

Perry now performs for huge audiences as a comedian. He has also been in Tyler Perry's films. Nevertheless he is very much a family man who has taken being a father very seriously all the way from the young age of high school to today. He is an inspiration because he took responsibility seriously while finding a ways to live his dreams.

Chapter 11:

Damon Wayans, Jr.

Damon Wayans, Jr. is the son of the famed Damon Wayans. Even though he has the name and star power of his famous dad and uncles, he is making a career of his own. He made his debut on Def Comedy Jam and is known for his roles in the series "Happy Endings" and as Coach in the Fox comedy series "New Girl".

What also separates Damon from the rest is that he is overcoming stereotypes about young men that are in his age range. He has shown strength and character as a young black male living in 2015. He is not a generalization or a statistic, but instead is defining the odds and making a career for himself that is worthy of his last name.

Chapter 12:

Christine Houston

Christine Houston is a woman who went back to college to prove to her kids that they could achieve and excel in life. Christine Houston did not know what she wanted to major in so instead she wrote a story and entered it in a writing contest. To her surprise, she won the contest. Later on Marla Gibbs, who portrayed the sassy and funny maid on the show, "The Jeffersons", used the story and script for,"227 ".

Christine Houston would continue to

write for the sitcom and also for the sitcom, "Punky Brewster".

Later on in life, Christine's husband would develop Alzheimer's. So she decided to write a book about him. The book is entitled, <u>Laughing Through the Tears</u>. Once while in a hotel, Christine saw her husband had left his shoes which she thought was strange. She soon went to look for him and found him sitting stark naked in the lobby. This was when she accepted that her husband had a serious disease. Living with her husband was stressful and she cried often until her son told her that instead of mourning over and crying about him while he was still alive, she should laugh at some of his funny antics. And so, the laughter ensued.

The laughter was not to mock him, but to find humor even though she was hurting for him. The creator of "227' is a woman full of love for family and her journey should inspire and help many people who have loved ones with Alzheimer's.

Chapter 13:

Paul Lamar Hunter

Paul Lamar Hunter is the nineteenth child out of twenty one children. His father, Mr. James Hunter, is survived today by his mother, Mrs. Eloise Hunter. His mother birthed 21 children and all were single births. When Paul's father died, his loss was felt deeply, not only because he was loved, but unfortunately for the family, financially as well.

Paul's mother became the bread winner or head of household and Paul's life was not an easy one. Even though some of his sisters and brothers were grown and out on their own, for him there was always the sting of poverty. Despite the difficulty, Paul, the nineteenth child, did excel. Even though there were trials and tribulations he is the first one in his immediate family to graduate college with a Bachelor's of Science degree.

Paul Lamar Hunter is an inspiration because he shows that none of us have any excuse not to be successful. Paul Lamar Hunter is not a statistic of one who just couldn't handle his life; he is victorious while still achieving and excelling as the nineteenth child.

Chapter 14:

Alexander Morton

Alexander Morton is Miss Black America 2014-2015. This pageant was established in 1968 by J. Morris Anderson. Anderson started the pageant to show that black women are beautiful and successful. The pageant is a distinguished and prestigious one that shows women of color in a positive light. Oprah Winfrey even wore the crown at the state level of this very pageant.

This pageant is the oldest pageant of its kind here in America. Alexander Morton wears the crown well and is an inspiration for many, not because of her beauty, but because of her grace and intellect.

Chapter 15:

Dr. Melanye Maclin

Doctor Melanye Maclin is a dermatologist who was on the, "The Steve Harvey Morning Show" and the weekly Saturday show "The Best of Steve Harvey". Maclin is also the writer for the Hair and Skin column in, *Hype* magazine.

This young woman is genuinely concerned about the hair and skin of others. She does research on products including her own. She is giving back to the community by providing support, information and solutions to problems with skin and hair. She helps men and women with a variety of skin issues and also helps supplement healthy hair growth. Dr. Melanye Maclin is helping a worldwide community to have healthier skin and hair.

Chapter 16:

Kevin Bion Spencer

Kevin Bion Spencer is a very talented American song writer and producer. He is also the lead singer for the group, Dynasty. Kevin has worked with and written songs for Leon Sylvers. Kevin was the driving force of Solar Records. He has written so many fabulous songs that they have been sampled by the likes of: Angie Stone, Shalamar, Luchini, Blaque, The Whispers, Carrie Lucas and the list goes on and on. Because of his gifts he has helped other young artists who are trying to get to his level. He has helped many artists' careers and is a well-known name in the entertainment industry.

Chapter 17:

Vickie Winans

Vickie Winans is a popular gospel singer. Her songs are inspirational ones like: "As Long as I Got King Jesus", "How I Got Over", "Shake Yourself Loose" and "I Already Have Been to the Water". Many people relate to her spiritual and uplifting gospel songs. But, what people may not know is that she also is a comedienne.

Ms. Winans is hilarious and has a comedy CD to add to her gospel line up. To add to that, besides being a gospel singer and comedienne she is also a great business woman. She has her own record label that produces her songs. She is definitely pulling her own wagon and is her own boss.

    Vickie is a multi-faceted talent and she is working just about all year long. She doesn't mind the work because she is the gospel while working. She is a role model to many people.

Chapter 18:

Harrison Page

Harrison Page is an actor who has had a long and impressive career. He has paved the way for many male actors and has opened doors that would have stayed closed if not for him. He did this by being one of the first.

Harrison is humble about his career and simply says, "I am blessed". Before there was a Denzel Washington or a Wesley Snipes, there was a Harrison Page first. He does not boast about his career, but encourages others to make the most of today's technology. He is best known for his role as CPO Sparkey and has well over a hundred films plus features on a variety of television sitcoms. He is still going strong with absolutely no reason to slow down.

Chapter 19:

Marc Gordon

Marc Gordon is a platinum recording artist, a member and also the co-founder of the group Levert. The group Levert consists of the late greats Gerald Levert and Sean Levert-- both sons of Eddie Levert who was the lead singer for the O'Jays.

Marc Gordon has also founded *SOEL* which is a public service foundation. This foundation's abbreviation means, "Saving Our Entertainers Lives". He started this foundation to bring more awareness to the drug use and alcohol abuse by artists and why they do it. Marc Gordon believes that there are too many artists who are dying because of the misuse of drugs and alcohol.

His goal is to save lives and bring more awareness to the stress and pressure under which celebrities live. He aspires to inform those who or close to them to see the signs of misuse and to intervene in their loved ones' lives to hopefully save them from themselves.

Chapter 20:

Mayor John Marks III

Mayor John Marks III is the mayor of Tallahassee, Florida. John and Jane Marks have a foundation that is entitled the *Jane and John Marks Foundation*. The main purpose of the organization is to improve people's lives through economic growth. It is also focused on educating people about technology through workshops. This foundation is closing the digital divide by allowing those to have access to laptops, computers, and other similar devices that might not otherwise find opportunities to do so.

Chapter 21:

Senator Alfred Lawson, Jr.

The former Senator of Florida, Alfred Lawson, Jr. was on the Democratic Party roster for the Sixth District. He represented the district from 2000-2010. He was also once a Representative for Florida from 1982-2000. This former senator is an alumnus of Florida Agricultural and Mechanical University, FAMU, which is a historically black University located in the state of Florida's Capitol, Tallahassee.

What makes Senator Alfred Lawson, Jr. a leader is how he gives back to the community. He even helped to build a multi-purpose center with a gymnasium. The purpose of the center is to offer free services from The Department Health. This center also has educational classes as well as Black History classes. The facility is 135,000 square feet and has a medical and athletic training clinic with a rehabilitation area. There is a computer laboratory that benefits the community as well. Thumbs up to Alfred Lawson, Jr. for giving back to the community.

Chapter 22:

Ted Lange

Ted Lange is an actor, director and play write who is well known for his role as the bartender Isaac on the long running sitcom, "Love Boat". The sitcom was on television for ten years. He has also been in numerous theater plays. Some of his plays are: "That's My Mama", "Mr. T and Tina", "227", "Fantasy Island", "The Hughley's", "Fall Guy" and "Lemon Meringue Façade" for which he received the Artistic Director Achievement Award. Ted Lange has also opened doors to give other actors chances to act and display their talents. Ted Lange is still opening doors and giving numerous opportunities to those who are trying to follow his lead.

Chapter 23:

Andy Hilfiger

Andy Hilfiger is the brother of Tommy Hilfiger who is a famed fashion designer. Andy Hilfiger is a trail blazer in his own right. He merged fashion and music and also worked with his brother on "Tommy Jeans" to make it a huge success.

Andy Hilfiger is humble and gives credit to staff along with others because he believes that no one makes it without help. He had a band and because of this he met musicians and artists with whom he could collaborate and include in the network with those with whom he made connections because of the clothes that his brother designed.

When he started his own company named "Sweet Pea Fashion", the first person he signed was Jennifer Lopez. Despite his wealth and fame, Andy Hilfiger helped with organizations that helped raise awareness and funds for issues such as, multiple sclerosis and autism. At the end of it all though, Andy Hilfiger will be known and credited for fusing music with fashion.

Chapter 24:

Dave Tolliver

Dave Tolliver was discovered by the late great Gerald Levert for the group Men at Large. When Gerald Levert and Dave Tolliver combined their individual talents they were symphonically unstoppable and wowed fans with their vocals. Dave toured the world and won numerous awards such as Song of the Year in 1993 and had platinum and gold albums along the way.

Mr. Tolliver adds many successes to his resume as he has also been in stage productions as well as being an R&B singer, songwriter, and producer. He even played Attorney John Baltimore in "Love's Triangle". He kept himself busy during any down time from his singing and acting by writing, arranging, producing, consulting, and implementing vocal training.

He has collaborated with other celebrities throughout his career like, Cuba Gooding Jr., Tommy Ford, and Darnell Williams. But one of the best things that he has done for himself is have gastric bypass surgery so he could lose up to 150 pounds towards a healthier lifestyle. This has inspired many and also and helped him to show others the importance of weight loss and health.

Chapter 25:

Dr. Willie H. Bailey, Sr.

Dr. Willie H. Bailey, Sr. is Vice President of Sales for Dudley Products, Inc., he is Vice President of Training and Recruiting for the same, he is Assistant to the President and Chief Executive Officer as well, all among other positions for Dudley Products, Inc.

Dudley Manufacturing, LLC is a company that does best practice hair care, skin care, and beauty care. The owner and president of the company is Joe Louis Dudley, Sr. Bailey, along with being Mr. Dudley, Sr.'s right hand man, is a board member of Kids 'N Technology (KNT) which is a company that was started to reward kids who made the honor roll by allowing them to build their own computers and take them home. KNT expanded to Vanderbilt University in Nashville, TN, Oglethorpe University in Atlanta, GA, Depaul University in Chicago, Illinois, and many other universities around the nation. Beyond supporting high achieving students by promoting technological engineering and advancements for students, the main goal of this foundation is academics and Dr. Bailey, Sr. is a driving force in this corporation.

This company helps to close the digital divide for young people and allows many of them to compete in this technologically progressive world. This company is owned by Jacquelyn Thomas-Coburn and Freddie Coburn who have helped make Dr. Bailey, Sr.'s vision reach fruition.

Chapter 26:

Dr. Walter Burns

Dr. Walter Burns is a distinguished Pastor of Southside Baptist Network. He is married to First Lady Deborah Copeland Burns. Dr. Burns has a Ph.D. in Clinical Child and Forensic Psychology and also a Ph.D. in Theological Studies. He even has a Master's of Divinity from Morehouse College of Religion. Dr. Burns is also formerly Magistrate Burns, a Judge at Fulton County Juvenile Court.

Dr. Burns is a member of President Barack Obama's Kitchen Cabinet and was appointed by

Official Commission in 2009 for this position in advisory to President Obama. This historical cabinet was created by President Andrew Jackson in the 1800's.

However, what makes Dr. Burns outstanding is his book <u>The Use of the Concept of New Identity in Christian Counseling for Sexual Addiction in Young Men</u>. In this book he addresses the young male, specifically those centered in sexual addiction. Not only is he addressing this demographic, but he is also teaching them how to become better men via Christian counseling. Dr. Burns is a strong example of what a Godly man should be.

Chapter 27:

Dr. Torri J. Evans-Barton

Dr. Torri J. Evans-Barton is a black woman who uses her own fatherless experience to help other young people who have absent fathers. She realized early that she needed the love and protection only a good father could give. She felt that her life would have been better if her father had been present during her life as she was growing up. So she started the organization *The Fatherless Generation* (or FGF).

This organization reunites children and young people with their fathers. Because she experienced devastation growing up she founded and is also the CEO of *The Fatherless Generation* to help heal the brokenness that the fatherless experience does create. The foundation has helped almost 20,000 children through various peer groups and has also mentored over 222 fatherless children while reuniting 176 fathers with their children.

Torri has an M.S. in Bio Chemistry Cell Development from Emory University and also a B.S. in Chemistry from the University of Michigan. She is an ordained minister and a certified mediator. As if that resume isn't impressive enough, Torri has an Honorary Doctorate from CIPA University and Seminary in Philosophy.

Chapter 28:

Attorney Racquel Brown Gaston

Attorney Racquel Brown Gaston is a practicing lawyer, wife and mother. She is from Falmouth Trelawny, Jamaica. At age 14 she moved to New York with her mother and was upset by the culture and economics within the city. To survive the crimes that she saw she created a world of her own that only she could understand.

Even though she is a Lawyer, Raquel's husband encouraged her to pursue her passion to write. She was inspired through his support and wrote the book, <u>Deadly Instincts</u>. The book has many aliases and is a fast-paced urban drama with crime and love. Gaston herself did survive the streets of New York making her an inspiration to many others who are growing through trials and tribulations in life.

Chapter 29:

Eddie Levert, Jr.

Eddie Levert, Jr. is the oldest son of lead singer Edward Eddie Levert of the O'Jays. Even though he does not sing as his siblings, the deceased Gerald and Sean Levert, he is a powerhouse is in his own right. He mostly handles the business side of things, but he has numerous charities that he works with as well. He owns a record label and is very charismatic and active in the world community helping others by allowing them opportunities to achieve and excel. He is a memorable guest on my show, "Show Talk with Angela Butler".

Chapter 30:

James H. Costen, Jr.

James H. Costen, Jr. is the son of the former Vice President of Morehouse, Dr. James H. Costen, Sr. Morehouse is an all-male University within Atlanta, Georgia. Costen has entitled an institution the *JH Costen, Sr. Institute for Complicated Freedoms* in honor of his father; it is an institution that addresses the needs of formerly incarcerated black people who have paid their debt to society via prison and the church. It also focuses on the rising number of black women in prison.

JH Costen, Sr. Institute for Complicated Freedoms addresses the number of men in prison who are serving life sentences for non-violent crimes and also the concern of mass incarceration. The institute helps the children who are left behind because of a parent or both parents being in prison and spotlights support for those in prison for drugs or non-violent crimes. Dr. James H. Costen, Sr. first started this type of support and his son has continued his legacy.

James Costen, Jr. has continued to research the readiness of the black church for its previously imprisoned citizens and also the unfairness and discrimination within the criminal justice system for black men and women. He gathers knowledge about the lessening of black people here in the community because of incarceration and wants to champion anyone affected by any time served once released with the concern of employment, housing, social ability, and forms of identification. He recognizes and informs others about the one third of black women who are imprisoned for drugs or non-violent crimes and how the black church itself addresses this mass incarceration of and trend of the depopulation of its people.

Mr. Costen, Jr. wants to make people aware that in today's society the black community is bearing most of the incarcerated people here in America-- the "New Jim Crow".

James Costen, Jr. has spoken and lectured all over the USA and South Africa. He is a driving force for letting people know the unfairness of the criminal justice system. His institute *For Complicated Freedoms* is one that has helped and will continue to help a lot of incarcerated people and he is also helping to reform the Criminal Justice System. James Costen, Jr. is making a difference for those without voices and letting them be heard through his institute.

Chapter 31:

Quincy Bonds aka "Pookie"

Quincy Bonds aka,"Pookie" from Tyler Perry's "House of Payne" is well known for this character, but Q is not only an actor, he has his own company called "Phat Comedy". This company produces sketch comedy, improv, and standup comedy. *Phat Comedy* has been in business for twelve years.

Yet, what makes this talented actor and comedian so worthy of praise is his division of *Phat Comedy,* "Kids Comedy Korner". What makes his company so different is because it is for kids, to offer them a chance to learn standup comedy holding improve workshops for kids ages 6 to 19. These amazing and talented kids compete regularly and once they are competition winners they get to be in the hit television show, "Kids Comedy Korner". Q's company is in major cities in the USA such as: Atlanta, Los Angeles, and Toronto. Q Bonds stands out from the rest and his ability to care for kids, to help them have a future of showcased talent and prosperity is what makes him shine.

Chapter 32:

Grand Master Kraiguar Smith

Grand Master Kraiguar Smith is a tenth degree black belt in Karate; he is also a thirteen time International Champion in Karate. He is a twenty-one time Grand Champion, not to mention USA World Champion.

Kraiguar is a historian and biographer as well. He has defeated many martial arts fighters, such as: Benny "The Jet" Uriquez, Howard Jackson, John Natividad , Cecil Peoples, Steve Fisher and many others. He fought in the U.S. vs. Japan match in 1979 and is the first African

American to fight in a main event in Brisbane, Australia in 1980.

Yes, Kraiguar Smith has many trophies and honors that have been awarded to him, but what makes him so unique is that he founded *The Black Karate Association* as well as *The Original Warrior Association*. The latter association is not about him, but honoring people who are pioneers and inspirations to other people. The pioneers are sometimes even worldwide pioneers. He is an inspiration because he empowers others who have opened doors for us all. He has also founded, "The Black Karate Association".

Chapter 33:

Ready for the World

Ready for the World is an R&B and Pop group that became known in the mid 1980's and the early to mid-1990's. This band rocked the world with hit songs such as, "Oh Sheila", which earned them a place in the <u>Guinness Book of World Records</u> for being number one on the R&B, Pop, Dance, and Video Billboard Charts. These gentlemen also had other songs that were huge successes such as: "Tonight", "Digital Display" and of course the sensual and sexy, "Love you

Down". But in spite of their immense success as artists, the group took a hiatus.

They have been working in many aspects of the entertainment industry as writers and engineers among other parts of the industry. This group has influenced many up-and-coming artists and well established artists and band. Their legacy will be listened to for many more years to come.

Chapter 34:

Author ANTWAN BANK$

Author ANTWAN BANK$ decided to write professionally back in 2012. He is also the owner of PRINTHOUSE Books Publishing Company in Atlanta. He is a very talented and smart businessman, but what makes him really stand out in the crowd is his book, <u>Gate Key: Turning your High School Education into Millions</u> which helps inform parents and youth about other professional opportunities that are available outside of college. Mr. Banks also released <u>Prisons for Profit</u>, an informative read about the everyday criminal system, our economy, politics and how private prisons made housing inmates a billion dollar industry.

Chapter 35:

Lennie Orrell

Lennie Orrell is a minister, but you may ask yourself why he is so worthy of mention. There are a lot of ministers, but this minister is a former gang member. He is also is an amputee who has only one leg. He was actually injured in a gang fight. It took him years to walk, but once he did he grew so strong so that now he is a martial arts teacher and wins tournaments with other competitors who are not amputees. He doesn't even stop there because he also works with the police to diffuse gang violence and he even ministers to gang members. Lennie speaks to schools about how do recognize gangs and also to parents about signs to look for to identify any gang involvement.

Minister Orrell has taken his life and used it to help others to not go down the path that he did. He helps law authorities stop killings among gangs and when I asked him what made him stop that way of life, he said, "my daughter". His daughter was with him often and once, near Christmas she asked him, "Will you be here for Christmas?" His reply was, "Daddy will make sure to buy you presents". But, she responded, "I am not asking God for presents, but for my dad to be alive." From that point, he changed his life and gave his life to God. That is why he is a celebrity.

Chapter 36:

Carla Mills

Carla Mills is the television host of "The Mills Connection" on which she has won awards such as, The Black Street Award and Who's Who in Black Atlanta. What makes Carla special, however, is that she took the time to be on my show, "Show Talk with Angela Butler" to talk about her personal story as a survivor of melanoma cancer. The other names for this cancer are Kahler's Disease or Plasma Cell Myeloma.

Carla was diagnosed with this cancer in December of 2012. She was misdiagnosed at first and went for a second opinion after her first doctor told her she had a year to live. Later she had a stem cell transplant. Carla has worked all her life, but 6 months after becoming ill she was let go from her job. Carla had health insurance, but after being let go she was blessed with a hospital and case worker who helped her get a grant for medicine that paid $5,000 a month.

Carla had always worked and considers herself blessed with the second opinion with a doctor who said, "You do have cancer, but the good part is you are not going to die"—especially because the first doctor's diagnosis detailed only 12 months left for her.

Carla's stem cell transplant cost a quarter of a million dollars, but it made Carla a cancer survivor who tells her personal story to help others be encouraged and educated.

Chapter 37:

Isabelle Doll-Ncogbo

Isabelle Doll-Ncogbo is a dancer and choreographer who was the first female African dancer that danced at Sun City Theater in South Africa. When she first started dancing there was still apartheid on the continent of Africa. She says that she constantly had to prove herself because she is Black, female, and in South Africa. At one point she was asked to dance topless and refused.

She first visited America for the Olympic Games. She taught the daughter of Winnie

Mandela and Ex-President Nelson Mandela-- MA diva or father in Africa which is a name of respect not endearment. She has her own dance studio and she travels with her students worldwide. Isabelle said when she was on "Show Talk with Angela Butler" that her greatest achievement is that, "I am living my dream because I am doing work that I would do for free." She has also worked with Michael Jackson, Toni Braxton, Tina Turner, Usher, and Gladys Night.

Isabelle Doll-Ncogbo survived and prevailed within South Africa during apartheid and is living to tell her story and journey, so that makes her a winner.

Chapter 38:

Herman Dummon, Jr.

Herman Dummon, Jr. is the CEO of *Beautiful Men & Women, Inc*. Dummon is a Black American man who was incarcerated at one point in his life. But he decided to change his life for the better. Now he is a motivational speaker who is from New York.

Currently his company works with Domestic Violence Victims, whom I call survivors, people with disabilities, and ex-prisoners. Yet he takes it further than the ones I just named, he also teaches living skills, personal development, leadership, relapse prevention, anger and aggression management, employability and transferrable skills. He does not stop there because he also helps with life style, prison culture, and recidivism to influence personal awareness development, to decrease violence, decrease criminality and self-defeating behavior, and bolster self-esteem.

When he was on "Show Talk with Angela Butler" he said this, "I had to understand that I *made* a mistake, but *I* am not a mistake". He has turned his life around and is helping others with their own life changes.

Chapter 39:

Willie T. Clay

Willie T. Clay is a Civil Rights Activist who walked across The United States. He is the author of <u>The Big Walk</u> and at the time of the interview on "Show Talk with Angela Butler" he was known as the *Civil Rights Movement Torch*. He was awarded the honor by Rev. Fred Shuttlesworth in his hometown and asked to carry on the legacy of the Civil Rights Movement. Since then he has continued the quest for economic parity for Black Americans. He has dedicated his life to inspire and guide Blacks in America to invest and participate in the mainstream of what America's Capitalistic System.

    Willie T. Clay believes that integration was not a good thing because Black people during segregation owned more Black businesses than now. According to Mr. Clay, he has turned down contracts worth $200,000 to fifty million because it did not include Blacks. He is also trying to take the focus of the past for Blacks within America, to impellent strategies and capitol development for collective wealth. He talks about Skid Row, where there are homeless men and women who are mostly Black Americans and he is very determined to lead Black Americans into owning businesses and corporations here in America and not just working for them.

Chapter 40:

Innocence Project

Innocence Project is a non-profit organization that helps to exonerate people who are in prison or on death row to be freed by DNA. Even though there are 330 people who have been exonerated, there are hundreds who have not and deserve to be. Paul Cates is a member of the *Innocence Project* and he talks about the work of the organization.

According to him the average length of time people are incarcerated is fourteen years.

Of that number; 62% are Blacks, 30% Whites and 7% are Latino.

Daniel Anderson, a man from Chicago was set free after 27 years, his conviction for murder exonerated because of DNA. The work of the *Innocence Project* is to: exonerate the innocent, reform through the courts, improve the law, and to support the exonerated after their release from prison. The *Innocence Project* was founded in 1992 by Barry C. Scheck and Peter J. Neufeld at the Cardozo School of Law at Yeshiva University. According to the Innocence Project the main reason for most convictions is misidentification. The second reason is invalidated or improper forensic science. According to Edwin Grimsley who is the *Innocence Project*'s case analyst-- and can be found per the *Innocence Project's* website-- it is especially horrific when teenagers are falsely arrested and convicted and most that experience this are youth of color.

I give a thumbs up to the people and lawyers of the *Innocence Project* and also encouragement to keep going strong.

Chapter 41:

Maxwell Pickett

Maxwell Pickett is the youngest brother of the legendary Wilson Pickett who is now deceased. Maxwell Pickett was interviewed on "Show Talk with Angela Butler" on an episode honoring his brother. Wilson Pickett was an R&B and Rock and Roll singing artist. He also influenced many other major artists and groups. Some of them are: Bruce Springsteen, Aerosmith, Hootie and the Blowfish and Led Zeplin. Some of his songs that he sang are, "Mustang Sally", "In the Midnight Hour", and

"Hey Jude", but there are many more songs recorded by Wilson Pickett. He was eventually inducted into the "Rock and Roll Hall of Fame".

Maxwell Prickett, in the interview talked about Jennifer Holliday who was in the 2010 show. He also spoke about the words of his brother before he died and how he is carrying on his wishes and legacy. Wilson Pickett inspired many and he is the legend of "Rock and Roll".

Chapter 42:

Bryan D. Barton

Bryan D. Barton is a former St. Louis Cardinal Baseball player and current baseball player for the Southern Maryland Blue Carbs. In the interview episode from my show he discusses his book, <u>Mindset, Awareness, and Action</u>. He talks about speaking things into existence and also about children growing up to quickly. In this thought provoking interview he talks about awareness, advice and action. He also discusses how to develop a healthy enhanced way of thinking.

At the taping of this show he was on the Southern Maryland Blue Carbs. Barton also has played for the Atlanta Braves. He is the first athlete that I interviewed on my show. He also has major foundations worth recognizing that helped him like, *The Magic Johnson Foundation* which helped him to go to college. He now works with this foundation to help other young people. Barton believes that because the youth are our future and that society often takes their voices away, he must show them and tell them that someone cares. He also believes that letting them know that they count and that they are counted will make a difference. He discusses technology and believes that it has taken away thinking for ourselves and interaction with other humans while glorifying thug life instead of what real success, instead of showcasing the towns and cities society should see with the many businesses that have opened that deserve patronage.

His book is about not letting society tell us what to think so we can obtain control of our own lives. The power of imagination is championed through Bryan Barton because he knows that what allows kids to think outside the box is also that which allows people to have control of their thought processes. He believes that many people do not have the freedom of self-controlled thought process and that because of this many people do not become successful. He states that people have to do more than speak it, as his mother told him, they must envision their goals in their lives. He goes even further to discuss bullying on the show to make others aware that there are people who are scared and being traumatized by bullying and that it should not become the normal or our self-controlled thought will be in even more danger, our future threatened.

Chapter 43:

Jerrell Shearin

Jerrell Shearin is the owner of the *Shearin Foundation* which is a men's semi-pro basketball team within Atlanta, Georgia. They are also a part of the Semi-Pro Universal Basketball Association and the United Men's Basketball League. The mission that Jerrell has is to lead the Georgia Spartans, his other foundation into offering local and non-local basketball players an opportunity to show their skills. He also wants to allow basketball players an opportunity play at more professional levels. They work with the Universal

Basketball Association (UBA) to advance their careers to the NBA.

At the time of his interview with me, the Georgia Spartans were undefeated. Jerrell Shearin is doing his part to help showcase the skills of the basketball players and to contribute to the community; this is what makes him stand out from the rest.

Chapter 44:

Andrea Hoosman

Andrea Hoosman at the time of my radio interview her was not the Vice President of the NAACP for the Saint Louis County. But, shortly later she was elected. She is not only in the lead for Saint Louis County via the NAACP, but her region also includes Ferguson, Missouri. In the interview she discusses the death of Michael Brown who was eighteen when he was shot by Police Officer Darren Wilson and would be attending college not to long after his death. The officer was not charged and was essentially found not guilty of any crime. The US Attorney General did visit Ferguson, Missouri and talked with the citizens there, but still contributed no real support. He later resigned from his position.

Even though Ferguson, Missouri is over 60% Black, the police force is less than 1% of the same demographic. Hoosman says that tear gas was used on the citizens who were marching, supposedly due to vandalism of properties. People came from all parts of the country to march with the Ferguson Missouri Citizens and people like Andrea Hoosman continue to lead so that the march continues.

Chapter 45:

President D. Scott

President D. Scott is the current NAACP President for Charleston, South Carolina. D. Scott talks about the murders of nine Black Americans within Charleston, South Carolina. President Scott connects to this to certain current issues like those that address the flying of the Southern Confederate Civil War Flag. Scott says that the confederate flag means hate and meanness to a segment of South Carolina and she went on to state, "That saying that the confederate flag is not wrong is comparable to telling Christians that the cross means nothing."

As she focuses on the story of the shooting in Charleston of recent days, she acknowledges that Dylan Roof killed nine people who were at church and who prayed for him before they were killed. She speaks on the fact that calling Dylan Roof mentally ill is an insult to people who are truly mentally ill. She believes that the nine Black Americans who were killed did not live their lives in vain and therefore their death is not in vain.

The nine people who were killed are: *Senator and Reverend Clementa Pinckney, Sharonda Coleman-Singleton, Cynthia Hurd,*

Twyanza Sanders, Depayne Middleton Doctor, Susan Jackson, Ethel Lance and the *Reverend Daniel Simmons, Sr*. I too believe that their deaths are not in vain and that those representatives such as Ms. D. Scott can lead us to the truth through becoming enlightened in the reality of our society and speaking for those whose voices were and will be silenced all in the name of ignorant and deficient acceptance.

Chapter 46:

Author Tamara Pray Frazier

Author Tamara Pray Frazier wrote a book based on the life of her Coach Faye Baker. Coach Baker was in a car accident and when she came to from the trauma she realized there was no feeling in her legs. She also heard the doctor tell her, "You will never walk again". Coach Faye Baker did not give up, even though she was paralyzed.

Tamara had always admired her coach's athletic ability because she validated Tamara's own athleticism and was older. Tamara respected that she was also a coach for the school, so much so that she tried to emulate her. Coach Baker was not driving the van that she was riding in for her accident, but was asleep in the back instead. Coach Baker says that the hardest thing for her was coaching the young women post-accident from a wheel chair. She could not do a one-on-one with her team or demonstrate new techniques due to the way her life had been altered.

Coach Faye Baker is a woman who had always believed in God, so she did not give up on her God and she had a strong united family who loved her. Sometime later, she actually felt her toes move and eventually she did walk again. Coach Baker is the true meaning of the will of the human spirit and how someone can maintain this spirit with the support of family and a belief in God. With these strengths and her determination, Coach Baker walked again which should inspire us all and the book that Tamara wrote in honor of her coach is appropriately titled, "In His Own Time".

Chapter 47:

Ricky Jason

Ricky Jason, a Civil Rights Activist, also makes films and one of his films is a documentary about James Byrd, Jr. Byrd lived in Jasper, Texas, but one day he accepted a ride with three white men and they killed him. The way they killed him is that they tied him behind the back of the truck and dragged him three miles on an asphalt road. Two of these men were known White Supremacists. They then dumped his torso at a Black cemetery.

Mr. Dick Gregory, the first man to run for

President of America and a comedian, Martin Luther King, III, and Maxine Walker were all a part of the documentary. The three Caucasian men who committed the horrible murder are: Shawn Berry, Lawrence Russell Brewer, and John King. Later, because of his murder, Texas passed a hate crime law. But, they took it even further all the way to the Federal level so that the law to prevent hate crimes such as this applies to all of the American States.

Congress passed the act and it was President Baraka Obama who finally signed it into law in 2009. Then in 1999 Lawrence Russell was sentenced to death by lethal injection for his part in the lynching by dragging of James Byrd, Jr. Lawrence Russell Brewer was executed

Angela Butler

September 21, 2011. The good part in this is that because of James Byrd, Jr.'s murder there is now a way for Black Americans to seek justice through the act that was passed-- Black Americans can receive justice in the American Court Rooms. Mr. Byrd did not die in vain, because of him there is now a law that protects and discourages the murder of minorities.

Chapter 48:

Cordell Dean

He was born Cordell Dean and he is a rapper and poet. At birth he was left in the hospital by his mother and put in the foster care system immediately. His name was changed to Cordon James Haveron by his adoptive parents. From the age of two to fourteen he was molded by his parents in Fillmore, Utah. At the age of fourteen he began to study poets and writers such as, Shakespeare, Edgar Allen Poe, and Robert Frost.

In time he won contests as he perfected his rap skills considering that it is just another form of poetry. He even won a worldwide contest which had over 26,000 contestants. Soon after that he met the Wu Tang Fu Gang. Near the age of twenty he was reunited with his family and even though his mother had kept the other six children, all except him, he still loved her and is still growing and bonding with her. His sister even helped him to come up with a stage name which is SEVEN 2 Life. A couple of his songs are, "Execution of the Cheater and "Missing You". Seven 2 life is not a statistic, but a survivor and winner.

Thanks for reading; *Inspirational Celebrity Short Stories* by Angela Butler. Be sure to check out more titles from her and other PrintHouse Books Authors. Please leave a review we would love to hear what you thought.

Angela Butler

PRINTHOUSEBOOKS.com

Read it, Enjoy it, Tell A Friend!

Atlanta, GA.

Inspirational Celebrity Short Stories